I0756418

FINISHING LINE PRESS
www.finishinglinepress.com

Homespun Alchemy

poems by

Julie Martin

Finishing Line Press
Georgetown, Kentucky

Homespun Alchemy

ISBN 979-8-89990-463-9 First Edition

Publisher: Leah Huete de Maines
Editor: Christen Kincaid
Cover Art: Shelli Walters
Author Photo: Stephen Locke
Cover Design: Elizabeth Maines McCleavy

Order online: www.finishinglinepress.com
also available on amazon.com

Author inquiries and mail orders:
Finishing Line Press
PO Box 1626
Georgetown, Kentucky 40324
USA

Contents

Hearth

Let's Meet

in the pocket of the hand-me-down jacket
with the reindeer charm zipper pull,

inside the rolled-up scroll in a band-aid box
buried beneath the Russian Olive tree,

through the links of the fence where the basset hound
leans to get her velvety ears rubbed,

in the space between the wall and the radiator,
where a Saint Bridget prayer card cloisters,

counterclockwise on the whorl of a baby's head,
on the same spiral that swirls through our galaxy

on the fulcrum of the red handled pliers that hang
in the chalked tool outline over my father's workbench,

beyond the surrender of each choice
in realms we have yet to imagine.

Anima Mundi

It gives ballast through the day,
this piece of unobtrusive umber basalt
found on the Keweenaw Peninsula,
hidden in my pocket.

Fingertips crave the texture
of amygdaloidal vesicles.
Pressed against a palm, it registers
eroded roots of mountains.

Songs of tumult and upheaval
resonate through my bones.
Memories of tribulations—
under pressure, liquefied by intense heat,
erupted from Earth's core.

Examined in light,
silver crystalline flecks glisten
and elements have tunneled
through the unyielding surface.

Hagstones, what ancient people
called rocks with natural holes,
believing the rocks possessed power
to heal, to ward off evil, and peering
through the aperture, imbued the finder
with openings into other dimensions.

Candle Scrying

Flame of fire
Flame of light
Bring to me second sight.
Bless me, help me see
The answers that are right for me.
—Traditional Candle Scrying Chant

Gaze until you become transfixed
on the flame that consumes all thought.
As it burns down, the candle's clove scent
curls into recesses of memory.

Give yourself to this light,
some seeds only break open under fire's duress.
In the clearing, from the destruction,
flowers will proliferate.

Follow the flicker between orange and blue
to the space between spaces,
to the recesses of the heart.
At the junction of gaze and flame

.
light splinters into myriad points—
A shimmer for every soul.
This flame is one and many.
Then it is just you and me.

Housekeeping

Because the kitchen windows are dirty,
she can't quite recall her grandmother's recipe,
yet the vintage cutlery of common sense
drop hints of dormant murmured incantations.

Marigolds blossom in the flowerpot of her mind
when garlic and onion splutter in olive oil.
Aromas riff across her taste buds,
a cello exploring the full depths of range.

Zucchini and pepper kaleidoscope-sauté,
while on the back burner,
farfalle pasta simmers, al dente.
She wipes her hands on a nonexistent apron,

and perceives the specter of Mrs. Lennon,
the original owner of this house. Long gone,
yet imprints remain, of a time when each room
was festooned with rosaries and prayer cards.

The "Hail Marys" she fervently uttered,
linger in corners, cling to fixtures,
disintegrate into generic grace
when at last summoned in service of providence.

Gray Matter

> *"Have you one gray hair?*
> *And does it frighten you?"*
> *—Ad for Notox "corrective for gray or white hair,"*
> *December, 1928.*

Gaze every direction, as far as you can see:
thunderclouds above, granite earth below.
Plunge the murky ocean depths, squint into
the diminishing twilight. Gray stretches
beyond what is known.

Turn inside. Follow the twists and turns,
the folds and crevices of the brain. Gray matters.
When I look in the mirror, gray hair no longer
concealed, my aura radiates silver.
Brushing the lustrous strands, I feel the dynamic tension:
pessimism and contentment coexist in gray.

Join the kinship of all creatures cloaked in gray:
spiders, moths, herons, dolphins.
The list goes on, past what we've named.
The axis of the color sphere—
gray is where all colors converge.

Between the thought and the word,
between the word and the page,
gray is the alchemy of pencil on paper.

It is with gray that you will leave your mark.

Darning Egg

Cradle it in your palm, smooth
maple, lacquered red.
Twist and split, the halves reveal a hollow
center for stashing yarn and needle.

Spun on the woodturner's lathe,
how many rotations did it take to arrive
at ovoid perfection?

Shift, turn, roll it from hand to hand.
Bare wood is revealed where
long ago, fingers wore lacquer thin.

Trail the grain with fingertips.
See the indentations where the blunt needle
tip landed? Imagine a bridge—
yarn spanning a raveled gap, wood
standing in for the shape
of human curve, heel of sock held
snug while fabric was mended.

I rub you for luck,
For a sense of how
to restore, mend, make do.

Catfish Jambalaya

With a towel slung over his shoulder
he sang while he did the dishes
in the kitchen's golden light.

As orange-scented soap suds filled the sink,
a few stray bubbles floated over his head,
a towel slung over his shoulder.

Rocking in a two-step he'd twirl the towel—
Me oh my! Oh catfish pie!
he sang while he did the dishes.

Drying the lids of the pots and pans—
Son of a gun we'll have big fun
in the kitchen's golden light.

Learning to Read:
1933 Elson Basic Primer

Inhabitants of the stories peek out,
beneath bright green vines that twine the cover.

Glowing from the center, the silhouette
of a boy astride a carousel horse
gestures to the reader to join the ride.

Gingerly, I turn the first brittle page.
A child appears, clad in a pink dress
with matching ribbons—my mother, six years old.

Her hazel eyes sweep across the lines, decipher letters.
She whispers each word through missing front teeth.

Absorbed with her task, she doesn't notice me
inhaling the faint vanilla old-book aroma
through the cracked hinge on the binding.

Eight Across

Steam rising from mugs of Sanka,
my parents unfold the crossword puzzle between them.
Double knit, her plaid pant suit undulates
as she places the well-thumbed dictionary on standby
for forays into unknown bits of knowledge.
Their minds intertwine as they bend over the task
of filling the interconnected black and white grid.

Each of them specializes in certain kinds of clues:
he covers sports and history. She brings a smattering
of French, Spanish and all the pop culture her *People*
magazine subscription supplies.
He adjusts the tilt of his head so his trifocals
bring the print into focus, reads the next clue aloud:
"Eight letters. 'Loyalty and affection'.
Starts with D. Ends with N."

Incantation for Ingenuity

My grandmother made scrapbooks from brown paper bags,
keen eyes focused, predatory scissors poised,
she quickly gleaned prints of domestic bliss,
clipping pictures of rosy cheeked children nourished
on soup and glistening towers of jewel toned jello.

Imprinted on my imagination, her curated images swirl:
color, empty space, bond of glue on paper.
The pages fan open in a dazzling display.

Omnivorous, her fingers would strut, foraging through piles
of greeting cards, magazines and calendars in search of whimsy:
kittens, ribbons, bluebirds, bells, posies, puppies, soda pop.

Sunshine in the rain, the yellow-frocked Morton salt girl,
glowed beneath an enormous black umbrella,
striding forward in patent leather Mary Janes.
A jaunty salute from the Cracker Jack sailor boy
offering up red-white-and blue boxfuls of the American Dream.

Lip-sticked, coiffed housewives, in high heels and ruffled aprons,
polished, scrubbed, vacuumed the household into nirvana
while the white wall tires on shiny new automobiles rolled
into the promise of spick-and-span tomorrows.

I grew up between the pages of her scrapbook, my first book.
A thousand eyes stared back at me
as I learned by heart—
          how to make something from nothing.

Devil's Ivy

Absorb energy from light, sentient being, son
of the westerly wind, Pothos in Latin.
Leggy vines, heart-shaped leaves climb, clamber,
twine through dreams.

Train-dancer, your shadow trembles on the wall
when the Amtrak Empire Builder thunders past.
Draped across the mantle, small dry nubs,
your aerial roots, adhere to the bricks
on a quest for the non-existent canopy.

You hearken back to tropical forests
where swarms of butterflies, ants and birds
were part of your birthright.

In exchange, you now occupy the space
between picture frames, lace curtains and swirls
of dust motes. Domesticated houseplant,
take every exhalation of carbon dioxide,

return it as a breath of fresh air, unfold
send forth pale new leaves, thrive
despite erratic watering, benign neglect,
you: a tangled infinity loop.

Upcycled

Black sweater,
thrift shop find,
damp, listless,
hanging outdoors
on the clothesline.

Cast off,
you have been revived
by traces of sunshine
absorbed into fibers
and the hallelujah of breezes
waving through your sleeves.

Were it not
for your backdrop
of darkness,
I would have missed
the glint of a spider's web,
illuminating filaments,
electric dots connecting
across your night-sun sky.

Ravelry

"Term derived from revelry and ravel.
A knitting or crocheting party or celebration"
—Urban Dictionary

Resilient, versatile, elastic, like spider's silk,
ink secretes across the page,

mind radiating out through strands
beyond the limits of the body.

Multiple lines cast into the wind,
carried upward by electrostatic currents.

Wait, see if any take hold. Follow one,
and then another to see where it leads.

Dangle on the bridgeline. Begin to scaffold,
secure anchor points. Dance in auxiliary spirals,
circle after circle of tenacious thread.

Tighten the filaments until the reverberations
become an extension of your senses,
a map of your memories.

The Writing Spider

Spiral orb web attached under the eaves,
a yellow garden spider hangs, head down.

The Turkish glass lamp of her abdomen,
yellow-black-white, illuminates the veranda
with southern hospitality. Silk zigzags
in her web glow in the sunlight.

If disturbed, superstition holds that
the writing spider will curse offenders
by scrawling their names in her web.

Hoping to get a better look, I blow into her handiwork,
oscillating the silken threads. She repositions
her legs, surfing this wave, rhythmically web-flexing.

I stand and watch, more blessed than cursed.

Opossum

I peer into morning's blackness as my breath
fogs the windowpane adding a halo
to the glow of the streetlamp.
Overnight, snowfall has covered everything
in undisturbed brilliance. The velvet brown
branches of the sumac are laced in whiteness.

Streets, sidewalks, rooftops dazzle
with the purity of a holy winter night. Inside,
on the verge of attending to the mundane:
feeding the dogs, making coffee,
preparing for the workday,

I almost miss the constellation
of tiny, star-shaped footprints
advancing across the front steps,
tail mark dragging behind

trailing winter magic in its wake.

Washing the Kitchen Floor

My mop twitches like a witching stick, glides
the wood laminate, hesitates beneath the radiator
where another layer of flooring is revealed:
70's earth-tones: harvest gold, burnt sienna,
coppertone orange, an interlocking grid
of squares and rectangles.

New, the bright colors must have exuded modern,
cheerful optimism, but now, the floor is worn, a relic,
a kind of dirty that will never come clean.

The mop twirls and augers down a century
below the wood laminate, below the vinyl.
What material was used for the floorboards
when this craftsman bungalow was built in 1926
and what lies below? Before the streets were platted,
named for clear-cut groves of trees, before the land
was graded, ground broken to lay foundations?

Groundwater, springs, fed by glacial meltways,
drained, diverted, paved over. Yet the water
is still there percolating far beneath our feet.

Estate Sale

Unfurl every linen,
lilac soap scented,
hand embroidered, too fancy
to use, every newspaper
clipping of "Hints from Heloise"
tucked in a ceramic bowl,
all the advice on removing stubborn
stains, how to make repairs,
how to make life easier,
cast off every garment,
faded, frayed, fleeting
moments trapped in fibers,
somehow the roses climbing
the trellis witness all
your comings and goings,
your joys and sorrows
enduring, despite this
liquidation of a lifetime.

This House, Embraced by a Maple Tree

branches above, roots below.
Stippled with moonlight, leaves
refract, benevolence over
the rooftop. Up the stairwell
my shadow splits, looms large up
the wall to the ceiling's apex, where
it respires, eclipses, reunites.
A leaf, adhered to the skylight,
spreads out in the sign of the hamsa
while moonlight bends off each
point, pools on the crown
of my head.

The Garden Gate

The Rambunctious Garden

Jerry-rigged with utility straps,
duck tape and bungee cords,
this gate is difficult to open.

In the flower box, plastic forks
defend succulents from squirrels.
Along the fence, raspberry brambles surge
rowdy and out of control in all directions

Towering in the raised bed, the lettuce
has bolted, run to seed, flowering and bitter.
Virginia creeper overflows the fence, into the alley
Everything calls for weeding, mending, pruning,

Yet I stand idle, watching pollinators
zip blossom to blossom, hoping for a glimpse
of a rusty patched bumblebee.

Antidote for Heartache

Account for all the different trees on this small tract of land:
blue spruce, red pine, juniper, maple, hemlock.

Create a mandala with twigs, berries, pinecones, purified air,
then stand back and watch as the squirrels testify.

Summon the spiders: cat-faced, starbellied, comb footed, wolf,
marbled orb-weaver, parson, recluse, jumper.

From silky filaments, classify the structure but leave the web undisturbed:
funnel, tangle, triangle, spiral?

Scan indexes of field guides. See if you can name your sorrow.

Helianthus

Look, the sunflowers
are reaching,
vying to outdo
one another

in the quest for light.
The tallest one,
first to unfurl,
reigns over the others.

Softly it hums
as gilded petals
scintillate,
"Stretch, grow,

spiral heavenward.
Offer up
your seeds. Transform
into goldfinch song."

Say it with Flowers

A little madness in the spring is wholesome . . .
—Emily Dickinson

Crocus, rose, marigold, cosmos,
Earth has donned her finery.

Heather, aster, lavender, ginger,
each petal beckons and beguiles.

Chamomile, bluebell, thistle, daffodil,
these dazzling stars, these radiant flowers,

Liatris, clematis, iris, narcissus
unruly, they shimmy in the breeze.

Columbine, snapdragon, bachelor's button, lupine,
toss their heads in the wind and laugh.

Agapanthus, amaranth, baby's breath, hyacinth,
coronas erupt in a haze.

Daisy, pansy, posy, ivy,
riddle at the bonds of domestication.

Chrysanthemum, trillium, geranium, delphinium,
stretch beyond the confines of the garden bed.

Petunia, echinacea, gladiola, dahlia,
trespass into the neighbor's yard.

Hollyhocks, phlox, four o'clocks
Each bud, a glimpse of the future.

Zucchini

To write as the squash plant that flourishes in the garden,
to scribble page after page, ideas sending out tendrils,
that issue out yet more ideas so prolific they yield mounds

of speckled, glossy green fruit. To hide beneath the broad-lobed
leaves mottled silver-gray and curving upwards to cup the sunlight,
to outstretch in mudras, complete circuits, guide the flow of energy.

To take up space, be a green growing machine, mansplay all over
the garden bed. To be prickly with fibers on pentagonal stems, leave
dot-to-dot rashes on the delicate skin of wrists and inner arms.

To send out blossoms of fat orange stars, male and female
flowers all on the same plant—his, hers, ours, theirs, then
leave it up to the bees to mingle the work of pollination.

Ode to Kale

Frilled edges fan out,
puckered, bumpy, leathery,
enormous. Delicate branching
veins streak violet through
crocodilian shades of green.

At first, no flavor registers,
this is a job for the crush of molars.
Each bite allows the release
of earthy minerals. I swallow,
and absorb its vitality.

Planted late last spring on the narrow
strip of earth between garage and fence,
you have flourished. Now, as the rest
of the garden succumbs to the desiccation
of fall, you remain, unfazed by frost.

Each morning you summon me to tear
off a leaf, place it on the tip of my tongue.
This is my body, broken for you. Take and eat.

Radish

Pale orb clad in crimson,
kith and kin of horseradish—
Cherry Belle, Malaga Violet,
flush with outside-pride.

A radish, eaten before bed
wards off gossip, marshalls
harsh words that could
form on the tongue.

Swashbuckling taproot,
accomplished crucifer,
ravish me with your peppery heat.
Relinquish your shadow magic.

Cobweb Hens and Chicks

Hair-like fibers grow on the plant and resemble spiderwebs.
Propagate a cutting in the window box of your imagination.
Study your aura for amplification.

A species of flowering plant belonging to the houseleek family.
Native to European mountains. Often found growing in rocky
outcroppings.

The ability to store water in their leaves enables them to thrive
in conditions most life forms find extremely challenging.

It's not what you look at, but what you see.
Hardy and adaptable. Spectacularly unneedy.

Low-growing, creeping succulents form mats around a common point.
These green rosettes produce pink star-like flowers and offsets.
The main rosette is the *hen*, surrounded by smaller offsets, the *chicks*.

After the rosette blossoms, it goes to seed and dies, then the plant
diverts its resources to the next generation. Each *chick* develops into
a *hen*, that in turn produces offsets and the cycle repeats in
perpetuity.

Some people hold the folk belief that hen and chicks possess magical
powers: When grown on the roof of the house, they ward off
lightning strikes. Protect the inhabitants from evil.

Placed In my garden, not on the roof, I fall under the spell of
the gossamer filaments that crisscross the tips of the leaves.

When I was small, my sister sent me to the narrow strip of land by the garage and instructed me to carefully watch the hen and chicks.

"Fairies live there," she told me.
"If you catch one, it will grant you a wish."

I am still watching.

Nessus Sphinx Moth

In the middle of June, running
my fingers through the tangled
vines of the potted Calibrachoa,
velvety trumpets of blossoms fanfare
in a cascade of purple-violet-wine petals
that decrescendo into midnight black
centers. Long stemmed, the tendrils
intertwine, sinuous curls writhe.

As I comb the unruly hair of this daughter
I never had, I explain that pixies tie knots
in your hair while you sleep, whisper
incantations in your ears, invite birds
to nest. Constantly working, my fingers
twine through the maze seeking desiccated,
shriveled blooms to snap off, making
room for new growth.

One of these deadheads vibrates under
my touch and when I spread it in my hand,
I find chocolate-brown, cinnamon wings,
two bright bands of yellow across the abdomen,
no longer camouflaged amongst spent flowers.
It thrums and vibrates, pulsates up my arm.

Bewitched, I watch as it rises, coiling
proboscis, flutter of wings, until all that is left
on my palm is a trace of its longing for nectar.

Advice From a Cicada

Absorb all you can from gestation
in darkness. Linger. Metamorphosis

cannot be rushed. When it is time—
molt. Cast off the shell

of former self. Emerge. Stretch
as rainbows of light
shimmer through new wings.

Find a tree that beckons you.
Make your way to the crown.

Align with pulses of the dogstar.
Bask until needles of starlight transform

into song. Rejoice.
Be relentless.

Stealth Manifestation

Flashlight in hand, I prowl to the outer edges
following the trail of clicks and whirs, trying
to catch a glimpse of the source of the sound,
that surrounds, heard, but not seen. Everywhere,
nowhere, its reverberations—an aural conundrum.

The next day, quest on hiatus, my son and I sit beneath
a canopy of trees on Summit Avenue. Silent. What
I have been seeking, a cicada, drops onto his shoulder.

Spindly legs climb aboard my extended hand, we observe
her from every angle: camo exoskeleton, lacy wings,
protruding eyes and an appendage—that I subsequently learn
is called an *ovipositor*—a tubular organ that female insects
use to first scratch a slit in a twig, then securely deposit eggs.
Perched on my fingertip, she has transmitted a clutch
of hope in crevices of my heart.

Arm around my son, I think of years spent underground,
before cicadas emerge, exulting songs from treetops.

Japanese Beetles

Overdressed, they descend,
gleaming copper carapaces,
jeweled emerald heads—
insatiable mandibles grind.

Through the raspberry bramble
wings whirl in a soundless blur,
coming to rest on the topmost bracts
to execute the task of decimation

laying waste to all that is tender and green.
No natural enemies, their greed
goes unchecked, leaves behind
brown skeletons for plants.

Predator, I have stepped into this role,
plucking beetles, sweeping them off canes,
interrupting the release of aggregate pheromones
dropping them in soapy water

in a jar that once held vitamins.
Its discarded label read:
For Energy! Immune support!
As I drop each beetle there,

I utter blessings of protection
for the plants, my own pheromone—
signals transmitting beyond the garden:
"Heal the world, make it a better place."

Grasshopper Blessing

O Grasshopper, visit my dreams,
show me new ways to be,
catapult me to higher realms,
bestir epiphany.

Long before the dinosaurs roamed
the fossil records show
Orthoptera made earth their home
millennia ago.

I conjure up your compound eyes
and your three ocelli:
with heightened sense, render me wise,
expand all that I see.

Hind leg and forewing stridulate,
the moon coaxes your song,
my intuition animates
and starts to sing along.

Bounce me into viridian
forward thinking hurdler.
beyond astral meridian
O Vibrant Reveler.

Blazon for a Banded Tussock Moth Caterpillar

Saucy minx, cosplay faerie
clad in a pouf of dandelion fluff.
Armored in multi-directional quills,
you venture into a hostile world

The foam rosette atop a latté,
you are the flourish on the forest floor.
Play of light, gray glimmering,
a ray of light in darkness,
the chiaroscuro of a Rembrandt painting

Voluptuous wink of a false eyelash,
you flirt, all wisp, vaunt and undulate,
sashay, blow kisses amongst birches,
hackberries and wild grapes.

An oak consumed, leaf by leaf,
reconstituted, turned inside out.
You are the robust dream
of an acorn come to fruition.

Late Self Portrait in the Style of Emily Carr

After Trees in a Swirling Sky

Hood cinched tight over a stocking cap,
only the small circle of my face is exposed.
Gloved fingers splayed, I ease down, unfold
my wool-clad legs on an expanse of beach.

Grasshoppers, revived from torpor in Autumn
sun, ricochet through leaf litter. Acceding
to gravity's pull, I lie down in sand
that shifts under the weight of my skull,
the jut of my hip bones.

Fading to glowing shades of gold, a cottonwood
shimmers above as I melt into the earth.

Approaching twilight

In the catmint
yellow-black stripes blur
in the pursuit of sweetness—
a sphinx moth's long tongue flickers.

Wild Bees

We search for
new nest sites
in shrinking pockets
of prairie.

The elixir
of our integrity,
is not for your
consumption.

Our work
is distributing
the sweetness
of this world.

Latham Raspberries

First came the longing for raspberries,
a rekindling of the instinct to forage,
lust for floral undertones, woody notes,
the goût de terroir of summer's peak.

Along hiking trails and bike paths,
in the alley, on the edge of parking lots,
across from Shul on the Hill,
a surge of elation at the cheerful pop
of red, vivid jewels, wild, unrestricted.

Vigorous, self-pollinating,
the raspberry canes I brought home
from Mother Earth Garden Center
flourish, require very little of me.

Is it possible to domesticate joy?

Raspberry Canes

In his favorite spot,
under the red pines
curled in a circle of comfort, my dog

watches while I prune raspberry canes.
Bent on the task of removal—
weak, diseased, spent.

With shears I twine
through the thorny tangle
of primocanes and floricanes.

Caught in the bramble
of my own thoughts,
my concentration is broken when the dog alerts—

his eyes flicker, nostrils swivel,
flews puff. With a tilt of his head
he summons me to join him,

walk the circumference of the tree's spread,
seek the source of a stuttering, staccato cadence.
First a black and white ladder back appears

through the camouflage of boughs,
then, a flash of ruby throat—
a yellow-bellied sapsucker drills sapwells, drinks xylem.

With fingertips on my dog's shoulder,
we give hushed attention to the bird's proclivity.
Each tap, an insight

into times the dog won't come when he is called,
but lingers under the pines, saunters over when sated,
coat stippled with pine needles

while his fur exudes the plush scent of all that is hidden in plain sight.

Observer and Observed

Ushering in from the north,
a mega-murder of crows,
subversively magnificent,
amass atop winter-bare trees
near the Basilica.

Glossy blue-black, highly iridescent,
the patina of feathers torque and reflect the urban
trespass of skyglow, pinwheeling charcoal, indigo,
periwinkle, violet, copper, gold,
dotted with pearlescent drops of moonlight

Foraging through the open dumpsters
of our lives, they extract hopes,
bottle caps, styrofoam, and secrets
like discarded french fries.

Behind those shiny dark eyes,
they know things.

Marvel

Stoked, hopped up on sugar sauce,
they poke their freaky, flicky
tongues in one thousand flowers each day.

Knights-in-shining-armor,
these flying jewels pierce the air,
gorgets aglint in the sun.

Less like Tinkerbell, more like Jaws,
open up wide like a catcher's mitt
and prey on mosquitoes and gnats.

Little bad asses
inhabit a realm nearly invisible to humans—
all we get is a glimpse,

of a whirling psychedelic blur.
Yet they possess SuperPowers—see colors
we can't perceive, off the spectrum.

Hummer Warz—they spin into aerial dogfights,
use their bills to fence and spar,
pluck feathers, defend territory.

They've got the moves,
twists, turns, maneuvers,
steep dives at break-neck speeds,
not afraid to embrace the dark side.

Big Rivers Regional Trail

Thoughts unspool as we enter
a rhythm of breathing and motion
in sync with our bike wheels,
scan the tops of dead trees
for silhouettes of hummingbirds,
tiny bodies perched, long thin beaks,
in optimal spots for flycatching.

As daylight fades, occasional gnats
in our eyes, we can only imagine
ruby-red throat patches, emerald feathers
in their soap bubble-shimmer.

Let us move through pockets of cool air,
let us wash our faces in the wind.

Regifting

A fairy garden concoction, not intended for me,
the gift was a hand-me-down from a friend

who eschewed this beribboned, bedecked
succulent topped birdhouse.

With no understanding of how to care for such frivolity,
I placed it between the rosemary and basil

where it would receive the same amount of water, sunshine
and lackadaisical care as the rest of the garden.

On a day when I was thinning radishes,
a blur flickered through the 'fairies only' portal.

Slowly, a long, thin beak emerged,
followed by a stout body vaunting a short upright tail.

With a flutter of dark, barred wings, it rose up
and perched amongst spent lilac blossoms

where this nondescript brown creature,
exploded into a jumble of bubbling song.

Birding-by-Ear

To learn the language of birds
you must immerse yourself

beneath rustling oaks and swaying pines,
while whistles and warbles zest the air.

Let the spice of each note swirl on your tongue—
cinnamon, nutmeg, cardamom, clove.

Be attentive to bobs and flaps.
Soon you will be conjugating chirps and trills.

As you discern cardinal from finch, wren from robin,
dark-eyed junco from black-capped chickadee,

pull out threads of song
to line the nest of your heart.

Minnesota River Bottoms

River and floodplain, the trail skirts
the bluffs, seven limestone blocks
engraved with the names
of seven Dakota nations.

A dragonfly divulges secrets
as it struggles to free itself
from entanglement in my hair.

Abrupt notes morph into trills
from the treetops. Some I recognize:
the *yank yank* of nuthatch,
okalee of red winged blackbird,
cuk cuk CUK shriek of a pileated
woodpecker, followed by the slow
resonant drumming of beak
hammering deadwood.

Like the threads of a vespers prayer,
my bike tires roll into the amber sunset.

We ask that you would open our ears
that we may hear your voice.

Autumn Coda

Periwinkle, the asters radiate,
pops of color, summer's grand finale,
beneath the blossoms, bees clasp to the stems.
Numb with cold, their dance has come to a halt.
Touch one you'll find, still it pulses with life.

Beyond

One of My Wishes

is that these dark trees
would allow me into their secrets.

When I retreat from sunlight
beneath cathedral like groves,
I enter the slow motion of tree time.

Electrical signals pulse.
As I eavesdrop, I am conduit
to their whispered messages.

Deciduous, coniferous—maple, juniper, blue spruce, red pine,
the shapes of their names
are the shapes of their leaves on my tongue

and I become a part.

Walk Amongst the Tamarack Trees

Knobby spurs of vivid green,
brush like tufts, tightly clumped, conceal
the understory, yet there are telltale
signs that porcupines have gnawed through
the tough outer edges of bark

like outdated beliefs, peeled away,
uncovering what is fresh and tender.
Continue to curve along this trail
of leaf litter, with occasional rocks and
sphagnum moss while layers of soft mud
kiss the lug soles of leather boots.

Dark clouds bruise the sky's azure-blue
but this perfect day will not be ruined
for, below, birds rustle and forage in flocks
shuffling on the loose ground
and, above, the white-throated sparrow's song
cuts an opening through the woods.

Catalpa Trees

I.
Go down the gravel road
past the farm where a family lived in a boxcar,
past the field with longhorn cattle
When you hear donkeys bray,
you are almost there.

Past fields of soybeans and wheat.
The wind will wave and part the stalks
revealing a rusted, abandoned truck.
Pull over where the fence posts meet.

Grass has overgrown the curb, but if you look hard,
remnants can be found, of a road that curved
up to the schoolhouse, all reclaimed,
by earth, wind and time.

Start at the catalpa tree, walk south in cadence
to threadlike echoes of creaking swings.
Imagine where the windows were, the cloakroom,
the pile of coal for the fire the teacher stoked,

This is the intersection between the past and the future.

II.
Some nights in dreams, I wander this space.
Though barbed wire obstructs entrance,
my uncle has the authority to enter.
With patient skilled hands, he unwinds
the wire from the post and ushers us in.

Large, heart shaped leaves sift the sunlight
as I scatter my father's ashes, upwards and outwards,
to consort with barred winged dragonflies
and rain down with catalpa blossoms.

Cherry Trees

> *The Dakota County Sheriff's Office is offering a $5,000 reward for information leading to the arrest of a serial tree killer whose victim list now includes 20 black cherry trees at Lebanon Hills Regional Park in Eagan.*
>
> —*Startribune.com*, March 2017

I.
On the steeps and turns of glacial moraine,
your soles bear muscle memory.
Your breath, cold March air,
footprints trail through hard-packed snow.

A labyrinth to others
you transect the forest
speaking the language of trees.
As they provide you with oxygen,
the leaves have left imprints
on your heart and lungs.

Leafless, gaunt in winter undress:
        oak, cedar,
        box elder, ash,
        black cherry,
        you say aloud.
Your shadow watches you remove
your gloves, span the trunk
with bare hands.

II.
Prepared with tools, knowledge, skill
you begin to cut
through plated outer bark,
past cambium,
into sapwood,
proceeding until you close
the ring,
        sever a complete band,
        choke the flow of nutrients,
        strangle the tree.

III.
Root systems connect, whisper
beneath your feet, each to each,
spreading your rot.

Above, clouds of breath plume, dissipate.
How will you be restored
to the expansive grace of the trees?

Samara

Scattered all over the tennis court,
maple seeds rattle and swirl.

Eddied by wind across the dark green surface,
a rosy purplish hue glows through

the wings of these papery angels,
known as *samaras* by botanists.

"Protected by God,"
Samara's meaning in Hebrew,

playthings, helicopters, to children
who delight at the way they spin, twirl,

disperse far from parent trees. These seeds
have landed on concrete, the wrong place

to germinate. All this potential wasted.
Across the net, my son, my samara, serves the ball.

I watch the trajectory and think
"may life carry you into optimal conditions."

Wetlands Psalm

Whose song is this that parts the air
atop the cattail reeds?
Backlit, so sleek, in morning light,
dapper rectrices preened.

Jet black the feathers, how they gleam,
lifted, they scintillate.
Epaulets flash yellow and red,
a pure voice resonates.

Each exhalation hangs mid-air,
afloat in cloudy mist,
the song suspended in vapor,
an unfurling spirit.

Breathe in a bit of this birdsong,
herald of Spring's return.
Absorb it in your heart of hearts,
let hope take possession.

Commute

East of the freeway
at 42nd and 4th
a lone wild turkey
forages through sooty snow
while my heart stirs aflutter.

Cove Point, Two Harbors, Minnesota

Cobble to cobble, boulder to boulder,
we pick our way to the water's edge
to watch the day melt into the lake.

A thin stripe of pink hovers over the tops
of evergreen, aspen, and birch.
On an outcrop of basaltic lava flow, billions
of years old, eroded by water, we sit

and wait for the waning gibbous moon.
As waves crash against the shore,
rocks clatter and chatter, chiming, lulling.

The reverie is pierced: swarms of mosquitoes
descend, intoxicated by the carbon dioxide cocktail
of our breath. Then a bombination of dragonflies
obliterate mosquitoes midflight.

We are delivered into a twilight glinting
from wings to water to feldspar crystals.

Borealis Chaser

Walk where eagles overwinter,
behold them, vigilant, watch them below,
swooping open waters as they enter

the river to alight on ice that's calved,
unmoored, broken from the shore,
they've surrendered. As twilight dissipates,

reach to touch the hem
of eternity's velvet gown billowing
plush blackness

undisturbed by light pollution.
Follow the trail of stars
as the sky undulates

in an impossible river
of fuchsia-green-lucent-white,
frost-sharpened swirling radiance.

Our muffled breath disperses
in bursts as the colors wash over
and ice crystals form on our lashes.

Ecotherapy

Oh dendrophile, oh lover of trees. Ruach.
Whisper this word that means *breath, wind,* and *spirit*—
graft the Hebrew into English.

The wind's trail is mapped on your fingertips,
ferns unfurl, nod and wave.
Pinecone bracts swirl future upstarts.

The woods crave your exhalations.
Sample the tang of balsamiferous air.
As it circulates through your mouth,

name all the scents you can trowel out—
crush of fir needles, kick of wild ginger,
umami of morels, lingering of cedar.

Shelter in the lacework of shadows
while lambent sunflecks rain down.
What do trees know that we do not?

Cross-country Skiing Offsets the Winter Misery Index

Herringbone tracks spring up
beneath the shadows of their skis
as they jounce on the camber
and propel themselves upward.

Pixie-like, they spritz past
scantily clad in Lycra tights
while the wind gavottes
with the tassels on their hats.

In the democracy of fresh air,
shuffle-glide, I plod along,
riding the rails carved in snow,
hypnotic, freight on the tracks,

the weighting and unweighting
of the scoot-stride-slide.
Toes locked into bindings,
yet heels exhilarate in liberation.

Prevernal

March winds poke
the garden beds, lifting
leaf litter to peek at
what has survived
winterkill, rabbit damage.

Though all is swaddled
in dormancy, tiny pulses
of life burgeon.

Soon, every leaf
will unfold, unfurl
wildly green.

I'm full of longing and can't move.

Oh Dogwood, Oh Vibrant Red!

Were it not for the blazing of your stems,
all would be awash in grey.

Tide us over, muster our courage
as the muddy earth freezes
and thaws and freezes again
while March winds rattle bare trees
and dirty snow piles slowly diminish.

We long for the harbingers of spring
so flicker brightly, fan flames of hope,

Wake us all from dormancy
that we might witness
the moment the buds first break.

Sage Creek Rim Road
Badlands, South Dakota

I ride in an exaggerated slow motion of a mime—
recent rains have turned gravel to sludge
causing mud to accumulate on my bike tires.

Signs warn of stampeding bison and prairie dogs
carrying bubonic plague. "This looks like Mars,"
my son murmurs, looking over the landscape.
We are entering another realm.

This valley used to be ancient ocean. Striated spires
rise—ochre, mustard yellow, cinnamon, umber.
Layer upon layer of fossilized animal remains
suspended in time. Bison graze in the distance.
My husband and boys bike ahead, vying to outdo
one another in feats of strength and endurance—
competition breeding competition.

Standing alone, I look into the mirror of panorama
toward an inner terrain—rocky and difficult
to navigate. Yet sounds of life surround me,
a continual cycle, ancestor to offspring: spring peepers,
low to the ground, but singing high. Meadowlarks swoop
in and out, flaring and fading. Annoyed prairie dogs
chit-chit exclamations, shaking from mouth to tail.
Cows murmur maternal calls to their calves.

Finally, the sound of my own heavy breathing
as I gain momentum on the wet gravel.

Cheyenne Canyon

Start on a path scoured by erosion,
scree rolls like ball bearings
under boots.

Switchbacks and a gradual ascent
give way to granite arising
abruptly through sedimentary rock.

Reaching the summit reveals expansive views—
sprawling city below,
a different angle on childhood.

Stop here and rest awhile,
back against a ponderosa pine.
Admire how tenacious roots

found purchase in ruptures of earth,
thriving despite habitat that fluctuates
from drought to flash floods.

Orange-brown scales of bark,
layered like intricate jigsaw puzzle pieces,
leave impressions on bare arms.
Sun-warmed sap,
butterscotch-vanilla notes,
seep into crevices of memory.

Jeffers Petroglyphs

> *"Stones have a spiritual essence which must be reverenced as a manifestation of the all-pervading mysterious power that fills the universe."*
> *—Francis Lafleche, Omaha*

"Listen to Grandmother Earth" heralds the sign,
at the portal to the ribbon of native prairie.

An outcrop of Red Sioux Quartzite stretches for miles,
red to white, lavender-brown, lilac, carmine.

The metamorphosed sandstone ranges and towers over
buffalo grass, little bluestem, and prickly pear cactus.

Stories etched in stone, symbols of human thought,
the beginning of recorded Minnesota history.

Ripples on the surface from an ancient Proterozoic Sea,
striations from glaciers, scratches, grooves run all directions

When evening rakes low angles of light, petroglyphs
appear—turtle, buffalo, thunderbirds, people.

Golden shadows play as light passes through.
Amberwing dragonflies shimmer atop bush clover.

Near the glyph known as "First Woman,"
well-worn sandals rest outside the rope barrier.

Barefoot, the visitor kneels, reaches through time
to place fingertips on the hand emerging from rock.

Ghosts in the Eucalyptus Grove

"Is it more foolish to chase a figment
or assume that our planet has no secrets left?"
—Brooke Jarvis

Footsteps churn fern leaves,
mud and sassafras into a continual
confetti cycle: germinate, thrive,
die, decay, give way to new life.

The hollowed log of a King Billy pine
garlanded with moss and mist now
a lair for the transverse stripes
that radiate in shadows.

Every crack of a twig is ripe
for a glimpse of Thylacine—
amalgamation of a creature: head of a wolf,
hindquarters striped like a tiger,
long thick tail of a kangaroo,
the size of a Labrador Retriever.

Also known as Tasmanian Tiger,
the last of its kind died in a zoo in 1936.
Yet of all the world's extinct creatures,
it has the highest number of supposed
post-extinction sightings.

Eyes gleam in the dark on the threshold
between dead and undead, present
and absent, remembered and forgotten.

The Last Living Passenger Pigeon

On Sept. 1, 1914, a Cincinnati Zoological Gardens employee found the lifeless body of Martha, the world's last living passenger pigeon, resting beneath her perch.

—Eric Guiry, "Why passenger pigeons went extinct a century ago" The Conversation, March 4, 2020

Men still live who, in their youth, remember pigeons. Trees still live that, in their youth, were shaken by a living wind. But a few decades hence only the oldest oaks will remember, and at long last only the hills will know.

—Aldo Leopold, "On a Monument to the Pigeon" Dedication speech for the Monument of the Passenger Pigeon, 1947

Once part of a multitude, she died
in her cage at the Cincinnati Zoo,
in September of 1914, just fifty years
a keystone species, billions to zero, extinct.

Once the most abundant feathered creature
on earth, how their masses blackened the sky.
The flock, a mile wide and hundreds of miles long,
undulated and morphed, eclipsed the sun.

A living wind, a thunderous roar
a biological storm, they descended in droves,
cleared tracts of forest as they foraged,
glittered the ground with pigeon ejecta.
Rejuvenation followed in the wake.
They were shapers of the ecosphere.

Now, her taxidermied body is kept
locked in a metal case on the 6th floor
of the Smithsonian's research collection,
brought out for special occasions like the current
"Objects of Wonder" exhibit. Her internal organs
stored separately in jars of ethyl alcohol.

You don't have to travel to Washington D.C.,
as you can see photos of her online:
close ups of her flayed, spatchcocked,

all her parts diagrammed and labeled.
Next, click on the 3D simulation
to rotate and view her life-like display,
mounted to appear as if she's perched.

Iridescent feathers on the neck and throat,
breast a cinnamon-rose fading to white,
wings mottled black and gray, her fiery red feet,
unblinking glass eyes. A ghostbird.

Old deciduous trees still remember, myriad feet
dancing on their branches like phantom limbs

Bison Don't Surf

They follow new waves of shoots
that burst from the ground each spring,
track greenery as it crests the landscape,
divine the next blade of bluestem.

Selective in their grazing,
they ruminate on freshness,
each mouthful a brushstroke
in the spatial mosaic of prairie.

They start to surf that swell, then stop.
Mouths, hooves aggregate,

tread in place, consume tons of biomass,
revert grasslands to their earlier stages,
force continuous sprouting,
engineer and intensify spring.

They gather in the thousands, move in synchrony.

Green surges up, passes them by.
Bison don't surf the wave,
they create it.

The Cost of Admission

Slip switch through time and space,
another type of freight, passing through
the former cargo terminal, now a museum.

You won't find the train ticket counter.
Nothing runs through here anymore although
twenty trains used to arrive and depart daily.

Wander the exhibits, curate your own story
of the Great Wild West.

Dust mingles in the petrichor of an imagined past,
mahogany cabinets exude mothball wisps,
Victorian mourning wreaths braided from human hair,
a semi-circle of ornate pewter button hooks.

Beneath the glistening jewels of the beetle collection,
butterflies are arrayed in black velvet cases, each thorax
pierced off center so as to leave one side undamaged.

To exit this room, you must walk under the behemoth
of a taxidermied bison trophy mounted at a height
that will cause you to tilt your head back.

Though his eyes are made of glass,
you will never move beyond the reach of his gaze.

The Genesis of Language

When we open our mouths,
word-fossils fall from the tips of our tongues.

Preserved in the amber
of our collective unconscious,

sounds echo-buzz on our vocal cords,
resonate through our bones.

A mystery, thousands of years in the making—
language's phonemes, graphemes, utterances

arranged and rearranged into lucid systems.
Each time we speak, ideas travel

on puffs of air that evaporate into clouds,
only to return as precipitation,

words raining down
in a world without end.

Found

After listening to "Helping Hand" by Yo-Yo Ma

I walk along wind sculpted hills
of white quartz sand to satisfy my curiosity.
Sandpipers play chicken with receding waves,
while they skim, slurp, probe the mud.
Jellyfish, stranded by the tide, glisten and wink.

A tank-like structure somersaults on the waves,
resonates against the rocks.
I stoop down to take a closer look:
brownish-green, domed-shaped helmet,
hinged carapace, spiky tail.

Not a living creature, but the molt
of a horseshoe crab. There on the beach
I leave a former version of myself
and journey on, renewed.

Picking Up Trash Along the Mississippi River

Cigarette butts, straws, bits of styrofoam,
I pick up the trespasses of consumerism,
pray that my trespasses be forgiven.

Glinting in the sun, a piece of metal catches my eye,
yet when I pick it up, it wriggles in my hand.
Nearly transparent, slender, elongated,
diaphanous fins flutter, an Emerald Shiner,
tossed onto the rocky shallows. Caught.

I cup it in my hand, admire the articulation
of its spine through its lucent body.
It has nothing to hide. Released back
into its watery realm, it catches
a current and disappears.

The Third Deer

Browsing amongst twigs and stems,
three deer startle at our footsteps, bolt north
towards the Minnesota River, a reliable passage
days ago when it was frozen over

but now a maze of floating ice chunks
and patches of open water. The deer
slip in, swim, then struggle to find footing
on the opposite shore.

Front hooves scrabble, scrape and totter,
for a spot solid enough to heft the bulk
of deer body back to safety.
Two recover, run up the embankment
disappear under the cover of trees.

The third continues to lurch and flounder,
desperate. We stand still and try to lift it
with half-assed prayers, until exhausted,
it succumbs and we shift from yearning
for survival to willing its suffering to end.

Georeferencing

Lake of the Isles, Minneapolis

He must be somebody's brother,
he must be somebody's son,

yet he is always alone
and his demeanor suggests a mind afloat

like a helium balloon that has escaped
the string that tethers it to earth.

Grounded, the park bench is his meridian,
the starting point from which all other places

can be measured, pinpointed, found.
A human sextant, he shouts

longitudes and latitudes,
coordinates around the globe:

"...Fiji: Latitude: 17°S, Longitude: 178°E,
Nova Scotia: Latitude: 45°N, Longitude: 62°W ..."

When joggers and walkers enter his circumference,
he pauses until they cross an imaginary line,

equidistant from a celestial body,
then he resumes, loud, clear, urgent,

as if others are depending on him.
Broadcasting, his voice drifts across the lake,

drifts across the city to the 45th parallel,
drifts across time and space,

navigating all of us home

Ungrasp

Fan open this book of feathers,
bedraggled green, iridescent blue.
Chant the incantation of extravagant beauty,
peacocks will roost in your dreams.
Hold a pebble under your tongue,
until your epiglottis hums of streams and rivers.
Construct an argument with a gilded pen
With each new paragraph, grope for words.
Accede to gravity's pull, become absorbed,
disintegrate into traces of minerals.

West Fork, Oak Creek

First there was the creek
with its many crossings—
steppingstones, fallen logs,
wind-polished slickrock,
the constant murmur
of moving water.

Then there was the balm
of the ponderosa pine's
butterscotch aromatherapy.

As the waning gibbous moon brushed
the tips of the giant sequoias
a wolf spider's eyeshine glittered blue-green
in the reflection of our headlamps.

All of this shimmering
cannot be captured or contained
yet I have committed it to memory
so I can bring it back to you.

NOTES

Let's Meet
This poem was inspired by Diane Seuss' poem "Let's Meet Somewhere Outside Time and Space."

Anima Mundi
Anima mundi is a term that comes from medieval Latin meaning 'the soul of the world.'

Catfish Jambalaya
Based on memories of my father singing Hank Williams' "Jambalaya". The original lyrics include *crawfish pie,* but my father's version featured *catfish pie.* "Jambalaya (On the Bayou),"
July, 1952.

This House, Embraced by a Maple Tree
The Hamsa is an amulet in the shape of a human hand, is a symbol of protection in both Jewish and Islamic cultures.

Ode to Kale
"This is my body, broken for you. Take and eat" (1 Corinthians 11:24) is said as part of the liturgy of the Eucharist, an invitation to receive Holy Communion.

Observer and Observed
Every winter thousands and thousands of crows gather in Minneapolis, known as the "Minneapolis Mega-Murder."

Big Rivers Regional Trail
The line—"Let us move through pockets of cool air, let us wash our faces in the wind"—was inspired by Ilya Kaminsky's poem "Such is the Story Made of Stubbornness and a Little Air."

Acknowledgments

A heartfelt thanks goes out to all the people who helped in the creation of this book: faithful friends and readers: Clare Welter, Patrice Pavek and Linda Wilterdink, River Urke; my writing group, The Monday Night Poets: Ruth, McArthur, Robin Greenler, Sharon Ankrum and Jan Stanton, the aunties of my poems; my teachers: Caryn Miriam-Goldberg, Freesia McKee, Caits Meissner, Sarah Sadie, LouAnn Shepherd Muhm and the many poets who have critiqued, given feedback and suggestions for revision. Fellow classmates of the Northbeach Writers Retreats; Birds Nest Poetry and of course, my family.

The following poems have appeared as listed (sometimes in a slightly different form):

"Advice From a Cicada"—*Plants & Poetry*
"Anima Mundi"—*In Want of Jasmine*
"Antidote for Heartache"—*The Coop: A Poetry Cooperative*
"Bison Don't Surf"—*Pasque Petals*
"Catalpa Trees"—*Dreamers Writing*
"Catfish Jambalaya"—*In Want of Jasmine*
"Cherry Trees"—*Plants & Poetry*
"Commute"—*Gravitas*
"Cove Point Two Harbors"—*Talking Stick*
"Darning Egg"—*Poetry Superhighway*
"Forest Homage"—*Green Island Poetry Walk, Poems, More Poems of Hope and Reassurance*
"Forest Homage"—*Moonshadow Sanctuary Press, Formidable Woman Sanctuary*
"Found"—*Thimble Literary Magazine*
"Georeferencing"—*Cedar Isles, Poeting the Parks; Agates*
"Ghosts in the Eucalyptus Grove"—*Writers Resist*
"Helianthus"—*Poetry Walk, Richfield Lake Park*
"Housekeeping"—*Cracked Walnut Journal*
"Incantation for Ingenuity"—*Optopia*
"Jeffers Petroglyphs"—*Plants & Poetry, Gravity's Grave*
"Marvel"—*Moonshadow Sanctuary Press, Formidable Woman Sanctuary*
"Nessus Sphinx Moth"—*Tiger Moth Review*
"Ode to Kale"—*Plants & Poetry*

"Pothos"—*Plants & Poetry*
"Raspberry Canes"—*Plants & Poetry*
"Ravelry"—*The Coop: A Poetry Cooperative*
"Respiration"—*Plants & Poetry*
"Sage Creek Rim Road"—*South Dakota State Poetry Contest*
"Samara"—*Nature Now*
"Sempervivum Arachnoideum"—*Plants & Poetry*
"Stealth Manifestation"—*Moccasin Poetry Journal*
"Upcycled"—*Poems of Hope*
"Wetlands Psalm"—*Tiny Seed Literary Journal*
"Zucchini"—*Plants & Poetry*

Born on a fault line in Anchorage, Alaska, raised at the foot of Pikes Peak in Colorado Springs, Colorado, **Julie Martin** imprinted on the natural world. She has made her home in Saint Paul, Minnesota near the confluence of the Mississippi and Minnesota Rivers. Drawing inspiration from the natural word, her poems invite the reader to join her in discovering all that is hidden in plain sight.

Julie's poetry has been widely published in literary journals, and she frequently joins other poets in giving readings in Minnesota and beyond. Julie is also host of Birds Nest Poetry, a long-running open mic on Zoom that draws poets from across the United States. Her poems appear in several dozen publications, including *Plants and Poetry, Tiny Seed Journal, Agates, Thimble Literary Magazine, Gravitas, Pasque Petals*, and other journals. Her poetry has won awards from the National Federation of State Poetry Societies, League of Minnesota Poets, and South Dakota State Poetry Society.

In between poetry, Julie's hands have a mind of their own, and she is often making something: knitting, crocheting, sewing, drawing. For the past 33 years she has been a first grade teacher for the Minneapolis Public Schools.

Julie feels called to invite readers to walk with her between her garden and poems. She believes in exploring the unexpected wild, across from an international airport, between freeways and urban sprawl. Not a pristine wilderness, yet an example of how nature finds ways to carry on despite human meddling, to thrive in our midst.

www.ingramcontent.com/pod-product-compliance
Lightning Source LLC
LaVergne TN
LVHW090535110826
845146LV00003B/1100